FOR
CALLIE ROSE
AVA
Love, GREAT AUNT
SHEILA

# THE JOURNEY OF THE SOUL

Written and Illustrated by
Victoria Jones

Radha Soami Satsang Beas

Published by:
Jagdish Chander Sethi, Secretary
Radha Soami Satsang Beas
Dera Baba Jaimal Singh
Punjab 143 204, India

Fifth edition 2004

11 10 09 08 07 06     8 7 6 5 4 3 2

ISBN 81-8256-044-6

Printed in India by: Ajanta Offset & Packaging Ltd., New Delhi-110002

This book is dedicated
to the Living Master,
Beloved Saviour,
Eternal Friend

For children everywhere who wonder about God and his creation. Here is the eternal, universal story that tells of the love expressed in every faith.

In the heart of every child is the seed of love and the innocent longing to know about God. May this story take you on a journey of exploration; a discovery of truth in all its simple wonder and delight.

May every child, of every race and faith, find inspiration in these pages -- an insight into our origins, the long journey of life, and the wonderful possibility of finding our way back to our common home.

ong long ago
in the very beginning, before even time began...
there was God and nothing but God.
There were no skies or planets,
suns, moons or stars.

There were no people or
animals or birds or trees.
There was absolutely
nothing but God....

God was a wondrous Ocean of Light called Love.
In this Great Ocean of God there were millions and millions
of drops of Light that were all fast asleep.

And because they were asleep they had no idea
how magnificent and shining God was. Each and every drop
was a tiny part of the Great Ocean of God. Each little drop of Light
was called a soul. One of those little drops is you!

After a while God willed the creation.
He sent forth a wondrous luminous wave of Sound and Light
from his own Being and made the entire creation from It.

He made skies, planets, suns, moons, and stars.
He made mountains, valleys and deserts, oceans, lakes,
rivers and streams. The creation was majestic and beautiful...
but there were no living things in it to enjoy it.

So God decided to put on a play,
using his souls as actors, and his new creation as the theatre!
God was the Director, and He named his play, "Life."

Almost all of the souls wanted to be in his show,
so God told them they could leave their Home in the
Ocean of Light and journey down to be
performers in the theatre of creation.

But there were a very few of the little souls
that did not want to go at all. They wanted to stay home
with their Lord. But He told even these to go
and enjoy being in his play, too.

Then he put a mark on each one of the souls
that wanted to stay with Him, and promised them
that one day He would send for them and have them
brought back to their Real Home with Him.

He told all the other souls that if they ever decided
they wanted to come back Home again, He would mark
them too. One day, through God's boundless Grace,
He would help them come Home, too.

And so it was! According to the wishes
of the Great Lord, all the little souls left their Real Home
and drifted down through many splendid and magical lands
until at last they were here, standing on the stage
of this world we live in right now.
The show was ready to begin!

The Great Lord gave every soul
a costume to wear so that each little drop of Light
would be dressed to play its part in "Life."

The soul's costume is called a body.
Every soul on earth has a body to wear.
The length of time that a soul wears a certain body
and plays that part in "Life," is called a "lifetime."

Some souls were given the bodies of plants.
Some were given the bodies of insects and reptiles.
The Great Lord gave some souls the bodies of fish and birds.
Some souls were given animal bodies....

And some souls were given
the most wonderful body of all – the human body.
With their body costumes on, all the soul drops look different.
But underneath their bodies they are still the same
little drops of Light and Love.

We all belong to the same family because
we all have the same One Father, God, the Great Lord.
We should always be kind, gentle and loving to every living being
because a soul lives inside each one.

All the living things that we see in the world
can be divided into five groups. If we could see them
on a ladder, it would look like this.

Humans are on the top step because we are
able to understand that we are soul drops, not just actors.
And because of a wonderful secret you'll soon discover...

Animals are on the fourth step. They are lower than humans
because they are not able to realize that they are soul drops.

Birds are on the third step. Though they are free to fly,
they are less clever than animals.

Fish, Reptiles, Insects and Worms are on the second step.
They are less clever than birds.

Plants are down at the bottom.
They are the lowest form of life. They cannot think
and are rooted to one place.

The soul is what makes the body alive,
and able to jump and run and swim and fly!
When the soul's part in the play is finished, the soul
leaves the body costume. Then the body dies,
and no longer lives, breathes or moves.

But the soul never dies!
Your soul is a radiant drop of God,
so the real you lives forever!

Do you know what happens to the soul
after it leaves the body costume? It begins a new lifetime
in a new body! It is given a new costume and another part to play
on the stage of creation! This is called birth.

A soul can be born as any living being.
One lifetime you may play the part of an apple tree.
In another lifetime you might wear the costume of a tiger or a swordfish.
Or you might play the role of an Indian boy... or an American girl.

It pleases the Great Lord to see each being cheerfully accept
whichever role He has given it to play in "Life."

The play of "Life" is like a great circle.
The soul actors journey round and round, from
body to body, costume to costume, playing different roles,
for millions and millions of lifetimes.

God has made his play seem very real,
so his souls completely forget that they are just
actors playing parts. Sometimes they worry about
what has happened and what will happen in "Life."
But God never worries about what happens
because He is the Director, and He knows
that "Life" is just a play.

God is happy to see his play beautifully performed
by his souls. So enjoy his show! Be happy and grateful
for everything that happens to you in his play. And whenever
a scene is sad or hard, remember you are only playing a part.
The real you is your soul, a perfect luminous drop
of God Himself, so his love, power and
greatness are all within you!

Talk to God. Feel Him shining inside you,
loving you and giving you all the strength you need
to play the part He gave you, courageously and well.
This is called faith in God.

If you will always remember Him and
have faith in Him, you will be happy inside yourself,
no matter what happens in his play of "Life."

When the Lord wants one of his souls
to come back Home, He makes that person
feel lonely deep inside, like something is missing.
This is the Great Lord's special way of reminding the soul
that its Real Home is not in this world,
but back in the Ocean of Light.

The reason the human body
is so special is that it is the only body costume
in which a soul can leave God's play forever
and return Home again.

God has placed an invisible secret door
in every human being! This secret door opens
onto a hidden path that leads the soul back
through the many magical lands to the
resplendent Ocean of God.

And just as He promised He would
in the very beginning, God sends his own Great Power,
Mercy and Love down into our world to find the marked soul drops
and bring them back Home.

This Great Power is called a
True Living Master and lives inside a human body
that looks like yours and mine.

But actually the Living Master is a wondrous
Wave of God's Being, who comes into the world only to
gather souls from the show of "Life" and take them back Home.
These souls are attracted to Him like bees to honey.

The Living Master tells us all about our Real Home
and fills us with love for God.

When a person really wants to return
to the Great Ocean of Light, the Master teaches him
how to do so. He touches that soul with his Own Soul, and
an everlasting bond of love forms between them.

He makes a faithful promise to
take the soul back Home.

He shows that person how to close his eyes,
sit very still, and lovingly remember the Great Lord.
This makes him forget all about his part in the play for a while.

His mind becomes so peaceful and quiet that he is able to hear
the wondrous waves of Sound and see the shining Light
of the Stream that flows all the way back
to the Ocean of the Lord.

One day
the secret door opens,
revealing the hidden path, within!
Thrilled, the soul steps across the threshold,
into the starry sky of an amazing new world!

Each day, the soul follows the
ringing radiant Stream of Sound and Light
further and further up the hidden path.

And then, in this refulgent realm,
something wonderful happens!
The soul beholds a stunning
and magnificent sight!

The Master's dazzling Form,
made of nothing... but the Stream of Sound and Light!
Dancing with joy, the soul dives in and is carried toward its Home
in the powerful swift current of the Master's Love.

The hidden path leads the Master and the soul
through many marvelous and magical lands, until at last,
they round the final bend and look up to see...

Off in the distance...
the welcoming lights of Home!
Overflowing with love and longing for God,
the soul rushes on, until it arrives on the
very doorstep of God, Himself.
And then...

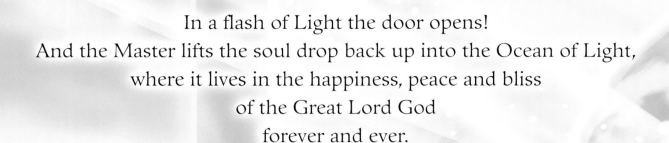

In a flash of Light the door opens!
And the Master lifts the soul drop back up into the Ocean of Light,
where it lives in the happiness, peace and bliss
of the Great Lord God
forever and ever.